WordPress Security Made Easy

Niko Guruli

WordPress Security Made Easy

VISUAL STEP-BY-STEP GUIDE FROM ZERO TO HERO

HOW TO INSTALL SECURE WORDPRESS SITE AND MAINTAIN IT

COST FREE AND WITHOUT TURNING INTO A GEEK

Niko Guruli

Quick Starter Books

Mgeli Press

Pasadena, CA

2017

WordPress Security Made Easy
VISUAL STEP-BY-STEP GUIDE FROM ZERO TO HERO

ISBN-13: 978-1546998723
ISBN-10: 1546998721

Copyright © 2017 Mgeli Press All Rights reserved

No part of this publication may be reproduced, distributed, or transmitted in any form or by any means, including photocopying, recording, or other electronic or mechanical methods, without the prior written permission of the publisher, except in the case of brief quotations embodied in reviews and certain other non-commercial uses permitted by copyright law.

Cover Design:
Mgeli Press

Print Formatting:
Mgeli Press

www.mgelipress.com

DISCLAIMER

This publication is designed to provide competent and reliable information regarding the subject matter covered. However, it is sold with the understanding that the author and the publisher are not engaged in technical, security of other professional advice. Laws and practice often vary from state to state and country to country, and if expert assistance is required, the service of a professional should be sought. The author and publisher expressly disclaim any liability that is incurred from the use or application of the contents of the book.

The author and publisher of this book and the accompanying materials have used their best efforts in preparing this book. The author and publisher make no representation or warranties with respect to the accuracy, applicability, fitness, or completeness of the contents of this book. The information contained in this book is strictly for educational purposes. Therefore, if you wish to apply ideas contained in this book, you are taking full responsibility for your actions.

The author and publisher disclaim any warranties (express or implied), merchantability, or fitness for any particular purpose. The author and publisher shall in no event be held liable to any party for any direct, indirect, punitive, special, incidental or other consequential damages arising directly or indirectly from any use of this material, which is provided "as is", and without warranties.

The author and publisher do not warrant the performance, effectiveness or applicability of any sites listed in this book. All links are for information purposes only and are not warranted for content, accuracy or any other implied or explicit purpose.

To know how to secure web-site takes years of learning and practice, right?

Wrong!!!

You'll see it yourself when read and follow this WordPress step-by-step security guide.

TABLE OF CONTENT

CHAPTER 1. FUNDAMENTALS OF WORDPRESS SECURITY — 1
- Why it Matters? — 1
- 3 Lines of Defense — 1
- Webhost Selection — 3
- Themes and Plugins — 3
- Importance of Software Updating — 4
- Safe and Secure Passwords and Usernames — 5

CHAPTER 2. SECURE WORDPRESS INSTALLATION — 9
- Why Manual installation? — 9
- Part 1. Creating Secure WordPress Database — 9
- Part 2. Create Secure Installation Package — 14
- Part 3. Upload the WordPress files to your server — 20
- Part 4. Access the Installation File from Your Browser — 21
- Part 5. Setting Up Administrator Information — 21
- Part 6. Post Installation Cleanup — 24
- Troubleshooting — 24

CHAPTER 3. WEAPONIZE YOUR .HTACCESS FILE — 27
- What is .htaccess file — 27
- Protecting Config File — 29
- Blocking or Allowing Directories by IP — 30
- Close for Public Your Directories — 32
- Turning off Server's Signature — 33
- Protecting .htacces File — 34

CHAPTER 4. MORE SECURITY MEASURES — 35
- Disable File Editor — 35
- Disabling PHP Error Reporting — 39
- Moving config.php — 41
- Don't Inform Hackers — 41
- Are Hackers Finding Your Username? — 42
- Don't make their life easier — 43
- File Permissions — 44

CHAPTER 5. PREVENTING BRUTE FORCE ATTACKS — 47
- About the Brute Force Attack — 47
- Google Captcha — 48
- Two Factor AUTHENTICATION — 51
- Installation — 52

Setup	52
CHAPTER 6. INSTALL & CONFIGURE SECURITY PLUGIN	**57**
Security Plugins, Why Wordfence?	57
Wordfence Installation	57
Wordfence Configuration	58
Basic Options	61
Advanced Options	62
CHAPTER 7. BACKUP AND SITE RESTORATION	**67**
Importance of Backup	67
What files Comprise WordPress	68
Backup Plugin Overview	68
Backup Plugin – Installation and Configuration	69
Connecting Backup to Cloud Storage	72
Mini Disaster Simulation and Recovery	75
Full Disaster Recovery with UpdraftPlus Free Edition	**76**
BEFORE YOU GO	**79**

TABLE OF FIGURES

FIGURE 1. NUMBER OF HACKED WEBSITES BY 12:10 PM.................................... 1
FIGURE 2. CREATE NEW DATABASE. 10
FIGURE 3. ADDED THE DATABASE... 11
FIGURE 4. ADD NEW USER.. 11
FIGURE 5. ADDED NEW USER. 12
FIGURE 6. ADD USER TO DATABASE... 12
FIGURE 7. MANAGE USER PRIVILEGES. 13
FIGURE 8. ADDED USER TO MYSQL DATABASE.. 14
FIGURE 9. ORIGINAL WP-CONFIG.PHP FILE. 15
FIGURE 10. GENERATING AUTHENTICATION KEYS... 17
FIGURE 11. CONFIGURING AUTHENTICATION KEYS....................................... 18
FIGURE 12. PREPARING ZIP FILE OF INSTALLATION PACKAGE. 20
FIGURE 13. ACCESSING /PUBLIC_HTML/ DIRECTORY..................................... 21
FIGURE 14. SETTING UP ADMINISTRATIVE INFORMATION. 22
FIGURE 15. WORDPRESS DASHBOARD. 23
FIGURE 16. ACCESSING WP-CONFIG.PHP FILE. 29
FIGURE 17. PROTECTING CONFIG.PHP FILE. 30
FIGURE 18. ACCESSING DIRECTORIES.. 32
FIGURE 19. THE TWO AREAS FOR EDITING PHP CODE. 36
FIGURE 20. DISABLING EDITING FROM CONFIG.PHP FILE. 37
FIGURE 21. AFTER DISABLING EDITING. 38
FIGURE 22. DISABLING ERROR REPORTING. 40
FIGURE 23. GOOGLE CAPTCHA INSTALLATION. STEP 3. 48
FIGURE 24. REGISTRATION FORM FOR CAPTCHA SERVICE.......................... 49
FIGURE 25. LOGIN PAGE AFTER CAPTCHA INSTALLATION............................ 50
FIGURE 26. INSTALLATION. STEP 3.. 52
FIGURE 27. SETTING TWO FACTOR CONFIGURATION.................................... 53
FIGURE 28. SELECT LOGIN SCREEN OPTIONS.. 54
FIGURE 29. REMEMBER YOUR DEVICE. 55
FIGURE 30. WORDFENCE INSTALLATION. STEP 3... 58
FIGURE 31. INSTALLING FIREWALL.. 59
FIGURE 32. INSTALLING FIREWALL, CONTINUED. 60
FIGURE 33. INSTALLING FIREWALL, CONTINUED. 60
FIGURE 34. INSTALLING FIREWALL, CONTINUED. 61
FIGURE 35. UPDRAFTPLUS INSTALLATION, STEP 2.. 69
FIGURE 36. CURRENT STATUS TAB... 70
FIGURE 37. REMOTE STORAGE CHOICE... 72
FIGURE 38. CHOOSING DROPBOX AS REMOTE STORAGE. 73
FIGURE 39. REMOTE STORAGE AUTHENTICATION LINK................................ 74
FIGURE 40. UPLOADING TO REMOTE STORAGE. 75

Subscribe for the mailing list and claim

FREE DOWNLOADS,

please visit the website of the book:

www.wpsecurityguide.com

CHAPTER 1. FUNDAMENTALS OF WORDPRESS SECURITY

WHY IT MATTERS?

I've seen different numbers, and by the most conservative estimate WordPress websites make up 25% of a total number of sites all over the world. Every day tens of thousands of websites get hacked, blacklisted or deindexed by Google, and presumably every fourth of them are WordPress sites. To put it in simple terms Google removes them from its search engine directories what means people can't search those sites. Go to website www.internetlivestats.com and check the number of sites hacked just today. I checked it at 12:40 PM when typing this paragraph and number was 40493 and the day was still young.

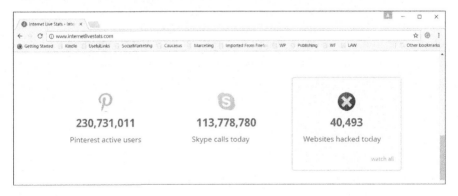

Figure 1. Number of hacked websites by 12:10 PM

3 LINES OF DEFENSE

This guide is about WordPress security, but you shouldn't forget that your website security is just a small part of bigger security system which you should always keep in mind. There are at least three lines of defense and if any one of them is compromised your security is worth of seconds that any hacker will spend before gains control over your website.

The first line of defense is the safety of devices that you use to connect to the site, that is your computer or laptop. If you perfected security of website but neglected security of PC or laptop, again it's just a matter of time when a hacker obtains all login credentials from unprotected device and overtakes control of your website. As you can see you can't feel secure if you are focused only on the security of the site. You should start with local devices. Here you can't, and shouldn't, ride free; you have to pay some money. The market offers an abundance of options. Do your due diligence and make a choice. I can provide only one suggestion, don't try to save a couple of bucks and don't buy all in one solution. You'll be better secured if you use separate software for different purposes, separate anti-virus, anti-malware, etc. Efficiency will be much higher. The principle of division of labor works even here. Make sure that all of your protectors are scheduled for the regular full scan of the system.

The second line of defense is the security of devices that you don't use directly and rarely think of, and these are devices through which you are accessing the internet, broadband or wi-fi router. Are they secured? Does a password protect them? Are they using any encryption to protect your data? Again, don't try by yourself to solve these problems. Better ask somebody who better knows what to do and what questions to ask your internet provider. Fortunately, this will be a onetime expense.

Only after you secured first two lines of defense, you can concentrate on the third one, the Security of your web-hosting company servers and security of your WordPress website. We will talk about web host selection and requirements and dive deep in WordPress security shortly.

By now you must be aware that securing just WordPress site is not enough, a threat of possible hack can occur at any lines of defense of your bigger security system.

WEBHOST SELECTION

Your third line of defense starts with your web host. Your web host has the responsibility to make sure your websites are up and running and are being protected best way possible. One of the most important things they can do for your WordPress site is to use most recent versions of PHP and MySQL.

One of the signs that web host company security wise is not reliable is falling behind in upgrading these two most important pieces of software. Most updates include security fixes of the software, and if web host company is not on the top of it, it neglects the safety of customers, i.e. you and me.

Find out what security measures they have in place against site hacking. Do they take backups? What about server maintenance. A well-maintained server is more likely to resist attacks. We all try to save some money, but host selection should not be the case. Be extremally skeptic with cheap hosts. You think you are saving money by choosing cheap hosts, but you are not. They will make you pay times more when you have problems, and with cheap hosts, you will have them a lot.

THEMES AND PLUGINS

The majority of security problems come with themes and plugins you install, that's why you must be careful when making decision about the sources where you are taking themes and plugins from. This is the case when free and dangerous are almost synonymous. But there is one place where you can get free themes and plugins with reasonable peace of mind. WordPress has its repository of free and secure themes and plugins. When any company or developer submits theme or plugin to wordpress.org, WordPress conducts its due diligence to make sure that theme or plugin is secure and complies with WordPress security standards. Only after theme meets all security criteria, they offer it on wordpress.org for free.

Don't use themes that add a link in the footer (or anywhere else) to any website. Only use themes from trusted sites. Besides WordPress repository, you can trust premium custom themes that have a good reputation, but this will cost you, and mostly it is worth of it. Keeping themes and plugins up to date is a must. Install upgrade as soon as possible, always. Otherwise, all your security efforts are futile.

But you have to be cautious. Free means that company has no obligations and very often no commitment for further development, maintenance, and support of the theme or plugin. You have to choose themes or plugins with some rating. Also, check feedbacks from users. Check how many people are using it, and what is critical, when last time theme or plugin was upgraded. Also, it's a good idea to check if the support is available and check how often and how quickly, if at all, are they responding to customers.

Never use plugins that link to another site from your site. Use as few plugins as possible. Be wary of plugins that are not well maintained. If you deactivate a plugin, delete it altogether. Often, even deactivated plugin is a source of threat to your site.

As you can see being safe with Plugins and themes as with passwords and many other parts of WordPress security is rather a matter of common sense than some technical skills.

IMPORTANCE OF SOFTWARE UPDATING

I already mentioned the importance of upgrades in the previous section. Just one more thing to scare you enough. WordPress has dedicated security team that works hard to keep our sites safe, and they do some excellent job. If you go to https://wordpress.org/news/category/security/, you will see Security Category Archive, where WordPress informs its community about security updates. Open any of these releases, and you'll see that every one of them starts with the following paragraph:

"WordPress 4.7.3 is now available. This is a security release for all previous versions, and we strongly encourage you to update your sites immediately."

What is most interesting and scary for you is that further WordPress always describes security issues being solved and thanks, reporters of the issues for practicing responsible disclosure. Guess who are among the most fervent readers of these releases? If you think hackers, you are right. So, now you can estimate your chances being hacked when hackers all over the world are routinely informed about security vulnerabilities of your version of WordPress site if you still haven't updated it.

The same logic goes for any software installed on your computer. Whether it's your operating system, or any web platform like WordPress or anything else. Most of us consider updating to be annoying. While that is true, even thousand times annoyance is better than the one-time damage that can be done to an outdated system. Hackers are studying platforms like WordPress and other popular CMSs and find holes to steal information or ruin years of work of other people. When updates are released, they are closing those holes, but hackers are finding new ones. So, this is really the never-ending race and to be on the safe side, you should constantly be updating your software.

SAFE AND SECURE PASSWORDS AND USERNAMES

Make your habit to follow these ground rules for password creation:

GROUND RULES FOR SECURE PASSWORDS

1. At least 12 characters
2. At least one uppercase letter
3. At least one lowercase letter
4. At least one number
5. At least on symbol character

Do not use the same password for more than one system. Do not use real words, names, birthdates, etc. The password should be absolutely random.

Use a Simple but Secure Algorithm

Do not use real words, many hackers employ brute force attacks, when they work by quickly testing random words. Using random strings of characters severely decreases the chance of a hacker getting into your system using this kind of method. Let's say you live on "245 Brand Av, Glendale, California". You could use 245bAgC#. I gave this example for demonstration purposes only. Common sense dictates not to use your real address or any address that can be somehow related to you. Chose an address that cannot be linked to you. Otherwise your "code" is easy breakfast for the hackers if they have some information about you. You can achieve more security by using a random phrase. For example, "We're just two lost souls swimming in a fish bowl." You could make from this wJ2lSsiafB&.

Do not use Admin as your username. It gives hackers half of the information they need to gain access to your website. Words like admin, administrator, etc., are among the first words they check. If you want an extremely secure password, then you must use Password Generators. The only thing to question is the generator app itself. Are they random? Are they safe? etc.

Some reputable generators:

strongpasswordgenerator.com; identitysafe.norton.com/password-generator; random.org/passwords.

Password Managers

There are different opinions on these types of applications. The biggest risk is if someone gains access to your computer, it will not be hard to obtain the passwords. There are local applications, more secure and less convenient – Keypass, Roboform, 1Password; and Cloud Based – less safe and more comfortable – LastPass. It is hosted on the encrypted server.

Avoid Dumbest Passwords Like These

- Yourname123

- Password
- 123456
- Abc123
- 111111
- Welcome
- Your name or kids names
- Your pets name
- Your phone number
- Your birth date
- Welcome
- Letmein

SIGNING IN

Phishing sites can replicate your page's appearance, so that you think you are signing into your domain, even though you may not be and just handing out your login credentials to hackers. Look at the URL in the address bar when logging in and make sure it is your URL if it's not your domain, don't log in.

Chapter 2. Secure WordPress Installation

Why Manual Installation?

One click or quick installation definitely saves time, is extremally easy and most of web hosts provide this service. But security wise manual installation is superior, gives you more control over the process and you are not dependent on your web host's preferences.

When you chose quick, or automated installation over manual installation, you are granting too much trust to your host. Because there are too many possibilities for your host to let you down. Does it provide secure enough password? What about database tables prefix, authentication codes, etc. There is a big chance that your host will fail you in regard of one, two or more security measures that you can easily configure when installing manually. And last but not least, during manual installation you are obtaining fundamental understanding of WordPress, what will be great help in the future, if you are going to maintain your site properly.

I divided this section in four parts to make it simpler and easy to follow step by step.

Part 1. Creating Secure WordPress Database

WordPress consists of several components. Directories and files on your web server and database that holds most of the content. So, the first thing to do is prepare your web server for WordPress installation, that is to create the database. For this purpose, you have to log in your account and access cPanel. It is extremally easy to create a database in cPanel interface. Once you access it and scroll down to databases section, you'll see MySQL Databases icon. Click the icon and this takes you through to the first step of database creation.

STEP1: CREATE A DATABASE

You need to create the database and give it a name. Depending on the host and specific plan you are subscribed to, you either create your username for server or host generates it for you. On most web hosts system will attach your username for the server as a prefix to your database name and database user. So, your database name will have following format: servername_dbname.

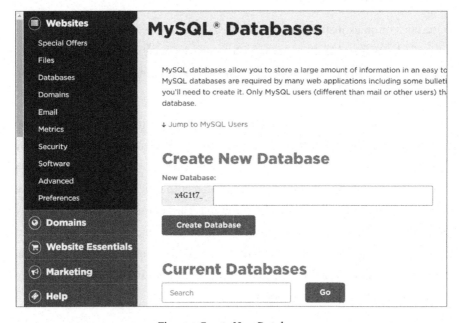

Figure 2.Create New Database.

Here, "servername" stands for the name you created or host generated for your account. "dbname" stands for a name you create for your database. It means, you just have to come up with only second part of the database name. If my username on the server is x4G1t7, then system automatically creates the prefix for my database as x4G1t7_ (Fig.2), and if I decide to name my database as DBcYv9, then the full name of the database will be: x4G1t7_ DBcYv9. After entering name in the filed click Create Database button. A message should appear saying: Added the database "XXX". In my case it says: Added the database "x4G1t7_ DBcYv9". Click Go Back button (Fig.3).

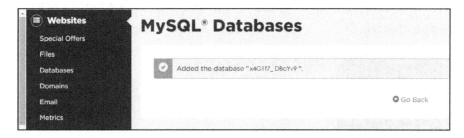

Figure 3. Added the database.

STEP 2: CREATE DATABASE USER AND PASSWORD

Scroll down to the Add New User section. For username, you have the same situation as for database name. Your database username format will be servername_username. The first part of the name is established by the system and is again your username on the server. Enter a value for the username. In my case, the first part of username will be again x4G1t7_ (Fig.4) and I have to come up with just second part of it. If I chose the name UNkT12, then the full name of the username will be x4G1t7_ UNkT12. Enter your username.

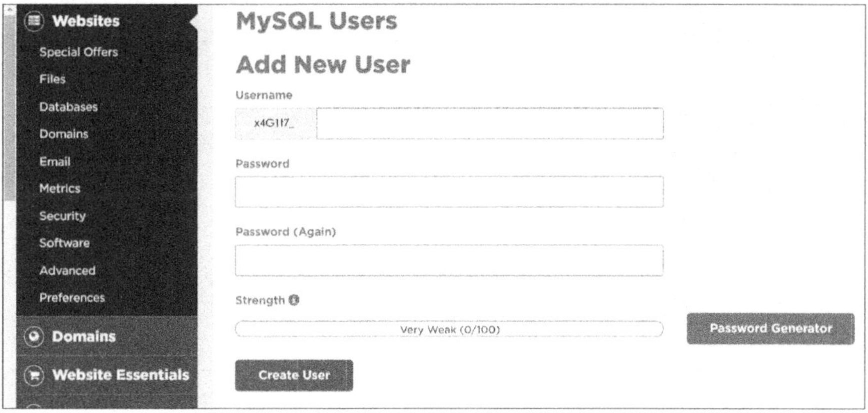

Figure 4. Add New User.

Next, you need to create a password. For the password, you need something really secure. I suggest using password generator. Depending on your situation you want to put it in a separate file and encrypt it for future reference. Enter a password and click Create User. You should get the message window saying: You have successfully created a MySQL user named "XXX". In my case it says: You have successfully created a MySQL user named "x4G1t7_ UNkT12". Click Go Back button (Fig.5).

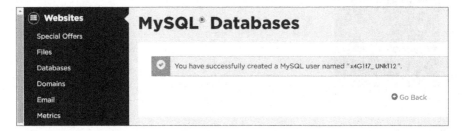

Figure 5. Added New User.

STEP 3: ADD USER TO THE DATABASE

Next step is adding the user you just have created to the database. Scroll down to Add User to Database section and click Add button.

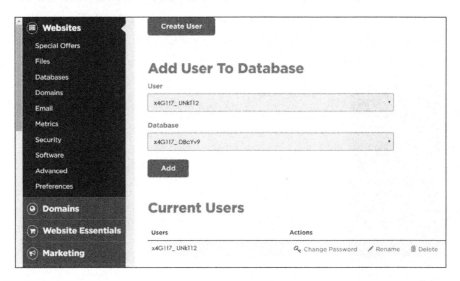

Figure 6. Add User to Database.

This takes you to Manage User Privileges section (Fig.7). Here, you have to create some privileges for this user. Since this is going to be the primary user, in most cases yourself, it is going to have all privileges. Some people argue that even for primary users it is a good idea not to give all the privileges, again for the security reasons. But when you add new users besides prime user (i.e. you) you should definitely apply Least Privilege Principle, that means you should give as less privileges as possible, just enough they need to do the job.

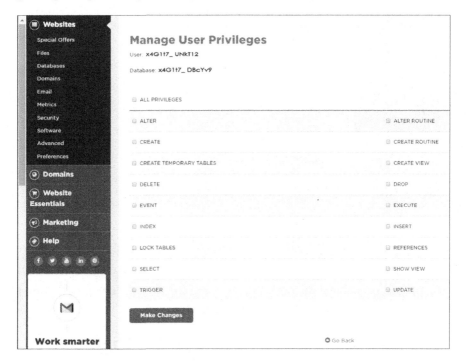

Figure 7. Manage User Privileges.

Since first users most likely are we, the owners, I'm always inclined to give myself all the privileges possible. Select privileges and click Make Changes button. You should get the message window saying: You have given the requested privileges on the database "x4G1t7_ DBcYv9" to the user "x4G1t7_ UNkT12". Click Go Back button (Fig.8).

This is all you need to do to create database and database user. From this screen, you can add another database, add another user to your MySQL database, or return to Home page.

From Database section of cPanel, you can click phpMyAdmin and log in with the credentials you have just created. You should see your database name on the left side, and everything will be empty before you install WordPress. Because you gave yourself all the privileges, you can see everything. Other users, if you create them, will see just what you allow them to see, depending on privileges you gave.

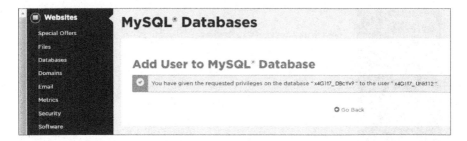

Figure 8. Added User to MySQL Database.

PART 2. CREATE SECURE INSTALLATION PACKAGE

Now when you have prepared your web server for WordPress installation, next thing you have to do is prepare secure WordPress installation package. You are going to execute this task in 5 easy to follow steps. Please note, that you are not just preparing installation package, you are already starting to add robust security measures to your soon to be WordPress site.

STEP 1. DOWNLOAD LATEST VERSION OF WORDPRESS AND EXTRACT

Go to wordpress.org and click Download WordPress button at the top right corner to download the newest version. Save zip file on your computer. Now you have to extract the zip file into the folder and do some magic for security.

STEP 2. COPY AND RENAME WORDPRESS CONFIG FILE

Find the file wp-config-sample.php. This is going to be the main configuration file of your website and we are going to talk more about it soon. Immediately copy and paste it in the same directory. Rename it to wp-config.php or, to avoid typo, just delete word "sample" and slash symbol. Now you have a wp-config.php file ready for use and original file intact. Let's open that file in a text editor.

Importantly not in MS Word or something like this, but in Notepad or Notepad++.

STEP 3. UPDATE DATABASE INFORMATION

First, you need to update database information in configuration file you have prepared in the previous step. In wp-config.php file find the line reading: //**MySQL settings – You can get this info from your web host **//. Here starts the block of the lines you must change.

```
wp-config.php - Notepad                                    —    □    ×
File Edit Format View Help
<?php
/**
 * The base configuration for WordPress
 *
 * The wp-config.php creation script uses this file during the
 * installation. You don't have to use the web site, you can
 * copy this file to "wp-config.php" and fill in the values.
 *
 * This file contains the following configurations:
 *
 * * MySQL settings
 * * Secret keys
 * * Database table prefix
 * * ABSPATH
 *
 * @link https://codex.wordpress.org/Editing_wp-config.php
 *
 * @package WordPress
 */

// ** MySQL settings - You can get this info from your web host ** //
/** The name of the database for WordPress */
define('DB_NAME', 'database_name_here');

/** MySQL database username */
define('DB_USER', 'username_here');

/** MySQL database password */
define('DB_PASSWORD', 'password_here');

/** MySQL hostname */
define('DB_HOST', 'localhost');

/** Database Charset to use in creating database tables. */
define('DB_CHARSET', 'utf8');

/** The Database Collate type. Don't change this if in doubt. */
define('DB_COLLATE', '');
```

Figure 9. Original wp-config.php File.

If you use Notepad++ it makes easier to find lines starting with word "define" they will be in blue color.

Find the line: define ('DB_NAME', '**database_name_here**');. You are going to put the name of your database which you defined earlier (Part 1, Step1), inside the quotes, in place of words that I made bold (of course it won't be bold in your file). Now the database line should look like this:

define ('DB_NAME', 'servername_dbname');.

In my case, it will be: define ('DB_NAME,' 'x4G1t7_ DBcYv9');

Now you need to configure database user name. You can find appropriate line right beneath of the previous one. It looks like: define ('DB_USER,' '**username_here**');. Do changes in the same manner, this time putting username between the quotes in place of "username_here" which I made bold. Now username line should look like this:

define ('DB_USER', 'servername_username');

In my case, it will be: define ('DB_USER,' 'x4G1t7_ UNkT12');

Next, you have to find the line "define ('DB_PASSWORD,' '**password_here**');." Here you put your database password in place of 'username_here'. Now the line should look like:

define ('DB_PASSWORD,' '%:24&fof1!T');

STEP 4. UPDATE AUTHENTICATION KEYS

Now scroll further down the configuration file and right beneath the database section find line reading:" * Authentication Unique Keys and Salts."

And further down you see the following block:

```
define('AUTH_KEY',              'put your unique phrase here');
define('SECURE_AUTH_KEY',       'put your unique phrase here');
define('LOGGED_IN_KEY',         'put your unique phrase here');
define('NONCE_KEY',             'put your unique phrase here');
define('AUTH_SALT',             'put your unique phrase here');
define('SECURE_AUTH_SALT',      'put your unique phrase here');
define('LOGGED_IN_SALT',        'put your unique phrase here');
define('NONCE_SALT',            'put your unique phrase here');
```

These are security keys and they were introduced in WordPress version 2.6. These keys add extra layers of protection to the WordPress site, encrypting vital information like passwords. If you look in your database which contains your password what you will see is an encrypted string. Because the password is encrypted, it makes all the harder for a hacker, who may have access to the database, to get access from that file. If you want to learn more about the security keys, you can find information on the codex.worpress.org website. As WordPress has evolved, more security keys have been added.

These keys are kept in the wp-config.php file. When you install WordPress using an automated installation software, the security keys are randomly generated behind the scene. If you install WordPress manually, as we do, you can use an online generator to create secure keys. Good news is, you don't need to remember them.

It might look and sound scary but really it isn't. WordPress made all this process very easy for us, all of non-geeks, to implement the process. All you need to do is to find URL which is given beneath the line: * Authentication Unique Keys and Salts and above of block of authentication keys and copy and paste following URL in browsers address bar: https://api.wordpress.org/secret-key/1.1/salt/ hit Enter and all the parameters missing between single quotas will be created.

Figure 10. Generating Authentication Keys.

You have to copy whole block and paste it in place of similar block in your config file. Now your authentication keys' section should look something like this:

```
wp-config.php - Notepad
File Edit Format View Help
// ** MySQL settings - You can get this info from your web host ** //
/** The name of the database for WordPress */
define('DB_NAME', 'x4G1t7_ DBcYv9');

/** MySQL database username */
define('DB_USER', 'x4G1t7_ UNkT12');

/** MySQL database password */
define('DB_PASSWORD', '%:24&fof1!T');

/** MySQL hostname */
define('DB_HOST', 'localhost');

/** Database Charset to use in creating database tables. */
define('DB_CHARSET', 'utf8');

/** The Database Collate type. Don't change this if in doubt. */
define('DB_COLLATE', '');

/**#@+
 * Authentication Unique Keys and Salts.
 *
 * Change these to different unique phrases!
 * You can generate these using the {@link https://api.wordpress.org/secret-key/1.1/salt/ WordPress.c
 * You can change these at any point in time to invalidate all existing cookies. This will force all
 *
 * @since 2.6.0
 */
define('AUTH_KEY',         'TS[.Xe[:-6|=&YH*>6)Z97b|~th&rDS.R{cc+p S)g0XB`Ze&upg5Li5HA]j.-Vi');
define('SECURE_AUTH_KEY',  ')|v5>h-OA6+ugMl8F7sKW0H!H| %[?R6by8tel[2Ra?#.wp-0;-CWc!sjiyl-Z}]');
define('LOGGED_IN_KEY',    'oKX/(lQv8H$v&Q:noc1(tD*g%zpWE~9|bd{[t-:2:R^2js$Skg`<_|2)->XPu_MJ');
define('NONCE_KEY',        'K2>M%.j|SGMgU<b.(c||&;JXz4vvy:965#Fhoc|/2b(XmUUV=yUYy]+{R&KFx$-]');
define('AUTH_SALT',        'SwC23j7mH4.d=uo:WLH;#4d].%5Go~K*MCNe9$@%r.f;u~#cI&(Dbj[.=QY.-"d!');
define('SECURE_AUTH_SALT', '(P0OTEhX{|=<UWD62(U9H)?AEH%# (G#E,T-(<T|5LS+x`=JF:KeK$6@8r|Yko4-');
define('LOGGED_IN_SALT',   'f?MG|NCJdI7b+v!0nG2+}K~d|c@d|E?z3hW&u(_`7eN&g/oo*x%a9-ADB-?G)z),');
define('NONCE_SALT',       'fD;ivyG-k[Wx.zX,cSXP.5OU.S$s|sS_H/ss+cKL}/|rMhX{boajx[L97+~jMl(A');

/**#@-*/

/**
```

Figure 11. Configuring Authentication Keys.

Of course, all this gibberish will be a bit different in your particular instance, but the general picture will be the same. A good security practice is to update these keys from time to time.

STEP 5. DATABASE TABLE PREFIX

Since WorpdPress uses a MySQL database consisting of database tables, to store your web site content, user data, etc., it's a crucial part of your site, and you want to avoid unauthorized access to the information in these database tables.

All of the tables that Wordpress creates when you install it are given standardized names. These names are identical for all WordPress sites, with the possible exception of a prefix added to the start of the table name.

WordPress by default uses the prefix wp_, and if you do not change this prefix, any hacker will know the full names (standard names plus prefix you did not change) of all your database tables. That gives them an advantage. For security reasons, you'd better do not give hackers any chance to guess anything. I suggest using upper case, lower case characters and number to create database prefix, as for usernames and passwords. For example, "tG5_". Slash is always needed, and you can't use symbols.

Scroll down and right after authentication keys section you'll find following line: "* WordPress Database Table prefix". Beneath this line there is another one reading: "$table_prefix = **'wp_'**;". You have to change these two letters as we have just discussed. Replace default table prefix and save changes.

PART 3. UPLOAD THE WORDPRESS FILES TO YOUR SERVER

You have finished preparation and before uploading WordPress package to the site we need one last thing to do. To make zip file of your WordPress package. In the folder containing WordPress files select all files (Ctr-A) and then right click >Add to archive...>Archive format | ZIP>OK (Fig.12)

Next, you need to go to cPanel and open File Manager to upload zip file you have just created. Find root directory on your website (Fig.13). Depending on your host it can be named as /public_html, or /www/HTML, etc.

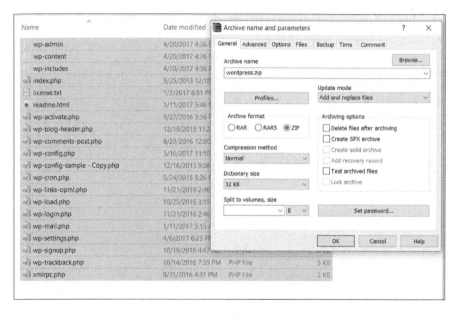

Figure 12. Preparing Zip File of Installation Package.

To power your entire website by WordPress you have to upload the package to the root directory. Otherwise, copy it to a different directory in your root directory. For this, you need to create folder WordPress or blog, or whatever you like in the root directory. In File Manager click Upload>Choose File and select zip file on your computer and start uploading.

When the upload is completed select zip file, you just have uploaded and click Extract in cPanel's menu bar. After the process of extraction is finished, you must see the same file structure as you had on your computer. For security reasons, it is a good idea to delete the zip file.

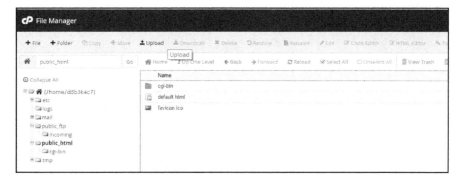

Figure 13. Accessing /public_html/ Directory.

PART 4. ACCESS THE INSTALLATION FILE FROM YOUR BROWSER

Now you are ready actually to start the installation process of WordPress. You do this by accessing install.php file which is in the wp-admin directory. You access this file by opening new browser tab or window and typing yourwebsitename.com/wp-admin/install.php and hit Enter.

What happens next is, behind the scene WordPress retrieves the database name, username, and the password you included in the configuration file, accesses your database and creates tables necessary to install WordPress. If there are some problems, and WordPress can't access files because you don't have the correct username in place or put something incorrectly in configuration file, it's going to tell you.

PART 5. SETTING UP ADMINISTRATOR INFORMATION

If you passed previous step without problems, on the next screen, you select the language you are going to use and click Continue. After selecting site language, install screen will ask you for information it needs to complete the process. You must enter site title, which you can change later. Also for security reasons, you must make sure that username you provide is not an "admin" or something likewise evident for hackers. Use some abbreviation related to your site. Make sure that you provide a really secure password. It must be a combination of figures, symbols, upper and lower-case letters, and not distinguishable words, or even better, use generated password.

Figure 14. Setting up administrative information.

Next, you need to provide an email address. Once everything is installed, you will be informed how to access your website. The confirmation email you receive will also contain your username and password.

And finally, you can allow your site to appear in search engines like Google. Or you can tick the box along Search Engine Visibility, in case you want to develop your site first before Google starts indexing it.

The last thing to do is click on Install WordPress button, and you have WordPress installed.

On the next window click on the Login button and it will take you to WordPress dashboard.

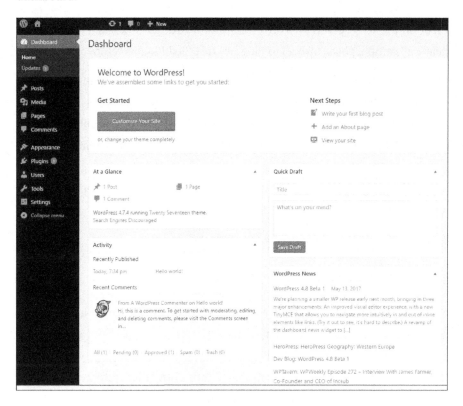

Figure 15. WordPress dashboard.

Now you have a brand-new WordPress site. And you can start customizing with themes and plugins and such, but the better strategy is to put in place certain necessary security measures before you start building the site. The last thing you want to do before going forward is to make sure that your site is accessible when you type in browser address bar your website URL.

Open new tab or window in your browser and type your website URL. You should get your WordPress site. In some cases, you might not see your WordPress site, don't worry and skip Part 6 and go to troubleshooting section and after you are done with troubleshooting come back to Part 6.

PART 6. POST INSTALLATION CLEANUP

The final step in WordPress installation process is just to do post installation clean up. Some of this cleanup you do in the WordPress dashboard and some of them on the web server. In WordPress dashboard, go to Posts>All Posts and delete all sample posts, also go to Plugins>Installed Plugins remove all plugins.

If you type in web browser yoursite.com/readme.html you can see that it immediately tells you, as well as to anybody else, your WordPress version. So any hacker who knows your WordPress version will know vulnerabilities of your site. So, you go to File Manager in your cPanel and delete the readme.html file. For the same reasons, you have to delete licence.txt. Next, you can go to the wp-admin directory and delete install.php file, because you don't need it anymore since you have completed installation.

This completes secure installation of your website.

TROUBLESHOOTING

You might need to work out one particular issue which you might have on your server depending on your hosting company. In many cases with some of the hosts, it could be an issue. If you go back to the root directory, you find the index.html file and this could be a problem. Index.html file is referred in the first order by the system and only after that index.php file. Latter is what will run WordPress. And index.html file is like a placeholder file your host put there. What you need to do in this case is to select the index.html file and rename it to index-original.html or something else. Now if you go back to the web site and refresh it you are going to see generic WordPress site. And you can start customizing it accordingly.

This is not the only issue you might encounter. Some other issues you might run into are install or database problems and other types of compatibility issues. But typically, WordPress is very easy to install if you have MySQL and PHP in place. Make sure you didn't make any mistake while entering your database credentials in the config file.

CHAPTER 3. WEAPONIZE YOUR .HTACCESS FILE

WHAT IS .HTACCESS FILE

The name of the file stands for hypertext access. It is important configuration file used by Apache Web Server and contains commands, also called directives. It is plain text file so you can edit it with Notepad or cPanel's built-in text editor.

By default, WordPress doesn't have the .htaccess file. If you go into WordPress installation most likely, you can't find it there. To get this file, you can create it manually or you can enable friendly URLs in WordPress dashboard, and it will be automatically created. This file can control a multitude of settings on your web server. Typical uses include authorization rules, authentication, rewriting URLs, control of directory listings, control file type and size, customizing error responses, etc.

This file is essential for your security and is processed by the server before any other code on your website. .htacces directives can stop malicious codes before they reach PHP code in WordPress. Changes take effect immediately. So, if you edit .htaccess code and save, changes take effect immediately. There is no need to restart web server or any services. Good news is that most of the web hosting companies support .htaccess files.

It's directory level configuration file, this means that it is placed inside the web directory where it overrides the subset of server's global settings for that particular directory where the file is located. Be careful when editing .htaccess file, this is one of the moodiest files you'll encounter when using WordPress. It takes only one character to be misplaced or missed for the code to be incorrect. When that happens, it may cause your website to become unavailable.

When you want to edit .htaccers file, always take a backup of it and store in the safe place on your computer. Whenever you update your .htaccess file and save changes, refresh your website to see if it's working. Don't skip this step. It's vital to verify if your site is still working correctly. If your site doesn't respond or returns an unexpected error just restore your .htaccess file. Upload backed-up copy and overwrite the version causing errors. Never forget: Make a backup copy before every change you make in this file!

Now, have a look at your page's link in browser's address bar, you should see something like this: http://yoursite.com/?p=123. You are going to change this. Not for security reasons but for display and SEO reasons. In permalinks settings, you can change how your page's URL looks like. In WordPress dashboard go to Settings>Permalinks. Most people chose Post Name so will you and click Save Changes button. If you reload your WordPress directory in cPanel or FTP, you will see that you have .htaccess file now, and if you still can't see it click Settings and tick Hidden Files box.

Download it on desktop and this is what you should see when you open the file:

```
# BEGIN WordPress
<IfModule mod_rewrite.c>
RewriteEngine On
RewriteBase /
RewriteRule ^index\.php$ - [L]
RewriteCond %{REQUEST_FILENAME} !-f
RewriteCond %{REQUEST_FILENAME} !-d
RewriteRule . /index.php [L]</IfModule>
# END WordPress
```

This is how the basic WordPress .htaccess file looks and all it's doing is allowing friendly URLs. There is not too much security in this code. But you can do a lot of safety precautions through this .htaccess file.

PROTECTING CONFIG FILE

Let's now address some security issues we can handle. First thing you need to do is to secure configuration file, wp-config.php file. If you type in the browser's address bar www.yoursite.com/wp-config.php, it's not going to show anything because it has no display (Fig.16). But in fact, you are accessing the file. To block access to it, you can just add a couple of lines to the .htaccess file. When you see # symbol, it means it's a comment. It's not going to be run or looked at or somehow executed. Just simple comment for yourself to remind what exactly this code does.

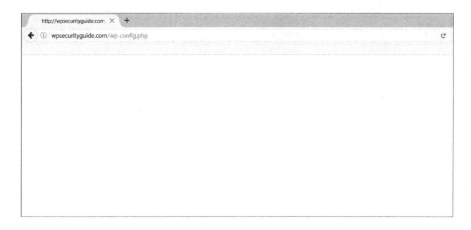

Figure 16. Accessing wp-config.php file.

Step 1. From File Manager in cPanel download your .htaccess file on your computer to make a back-up.

Step 2. From File Manager in cPanel open .htaccess file.

Step 3. Copy and paste from the provided file or type following lines into your .htaccess file:

Protecting wp-config.php
<Files wp-config.php>
Order Allow,Deny
Deny from all
</files>

Step 4. Save changes.

Step 5. Refresh the site.

After reloading the site, you should get the following message:

403: Forbidden

This page cannot be displayed.

In other words, now your config.php file is inaccessible. You can do the same with any file you want. Here is how your .htaccess file should look like after you add the code (Fig.17).

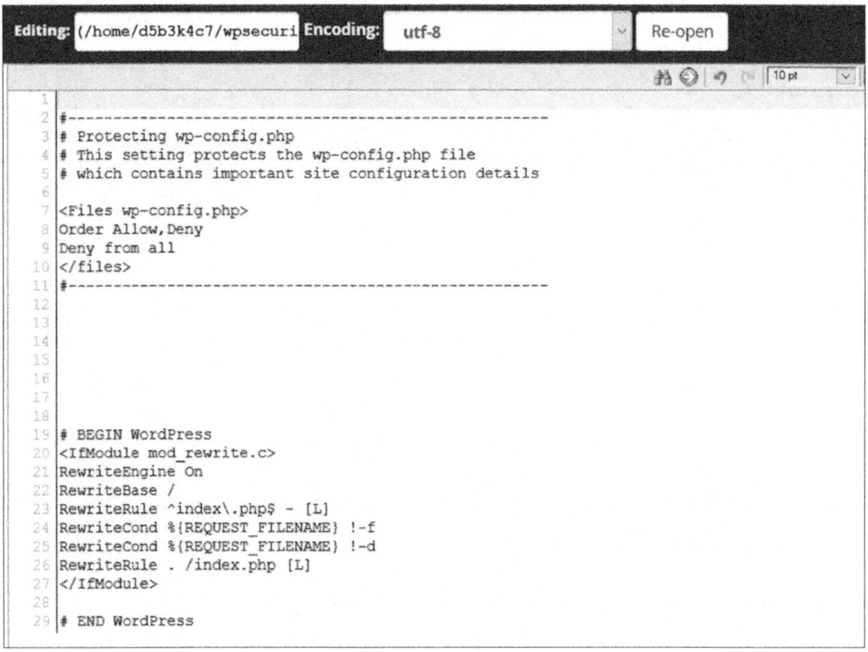


```
#----------------------------------------------------
# Protecting wp-config.php
# This setting protects the wp-config.php file
# which contains important site configuration details

<Files wp-config.php>
Order Allow,Deny
Deny from all
</files>
#----------------------------------------------------







# BEGIN WordPress
<IfModule mod_rewrite.c>
RewriteEngine On
RewriteBase /
RewriteRule ^index\.php$ - [L]
RewriteCond %{REQUEST_FILENAME} !-f
RewriteCond %{REQUEST_FILENAME} !-d
RewriteRule . /index.php [L]
</IfModule>

# END WordPress
```

Figure 17. Protecting config.php File.

BLOCKING OR ALLOWING DIRECTORIES BY IP

Go to WordPress admin page by typing www.yoursite.com/wp-admin, and you have access to your administrator login screen. The same can do anybody who knows your URL. Obviously, you don't want the other people to access the admin panel. You have the secure password, but you if you want to take security one step further, you can block entire admin area and allow access only to your IP address. This way only you can access it. Now let's see how you can prevent directories from browsing by IPs or allow certain IPs in certain directories. First, you need to know your IP address. If you don't, go to www.whatismyip.com and copy it and go through following steps:

Step 1. From File Manager in cPanel download your .htaccess file on your computer to make a back-up.

Step 2. From File Manager in cPanel open .htaccess file.

Step 3. Copy and paste from the provided file or type following lines into your .htaccess file:

```
#Restrict Admin Access
<Files wp-login.php>
order allow,deny
deny from all
Allow from xx.xx.xxx.xxxx
</Files>
```

Step 4. Save changes.

Step 5. Refresh the site.

Where instead of xx.xx.xxx.xxxx you paste your IP address. Now if you reload your site you'll be able to access it and nobody else. To test, you can change any one number in IP address and reload your site. You'll see that your admin area is blocked for you and only the person with IP address put in .htaccess file will be able to access. Of course, you want to go back and change back to your proper IP address.

This is superb security measure if your site needs that kind of security. But you should be cautious because as mentioned elsewhere, depending on your type of connection to the internet, it's possible that you don't have the permanent IP address. So, before you are sure about it put # symbol before every line of the code to disable it.

Note: Insert this code at the top of htaccess file. Also, don't be discouraged if it doesn't work as you enter it. Sometimes you need the change order of code lines, sometimes it helps to disable "deny from all" line by putting # sign in front of it.

CLOSE FOR PUBLIC YOUR DIRECTORIES

Let's look at something that is a bit scary. Type in your browser address bar your domain name, forward slash, wp-includes, and forward slash. It must look something like this: www.yourdomain.com/wp-includes/. Now, if you were redirected to your home page and nothing else happened, you are safe. But, if instead of your home page you are presented with the list of your files on your server (see Fig. 18), then you have a problem.

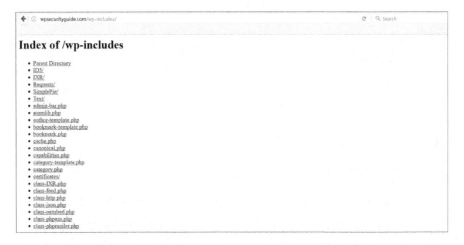

Figure 18. Accessing directories.

Your files and directories should not be open for public viewing. And that is what exactly happens when you see this particular list here. What you need is to add one quick line of code to your .htacces file. Many servers have this service in place by default. If your web host doesn't provide this kind of service and you like to be on the safe side you can do the following:

Step 1. From File Manager in cPanel download your .htaccess file on your computer to make a back-up.

Step 2. From File Manager in cPanel open .htaccess file.

Step 3. Copy and paste from the provided file or type following lines into your .htaccess file:

#Stop directory browsing
Options ALL -Indexes

Step 4. Save changes.

Step 5. Refresh the site.

This prevents any directory browsing. Save and check what happens if you go to the content directory by typing www.yoursite.com/wp-includes/. You won't be able to browse the folder. You should get the following message:

403: Forbidden

This page cannot be displayed.

TURNING OFF SERVER'S SIGNATURE

Another thing you should do is to turn off your server's signature. This is just the way to stop hackers from finding additional data regarding your server. This directive prevents displaying important server information in files generated by the server. Usually web hosts take care of it and disable this function but some web hosts may enable it, and better to be on the safe side.

Step 1. From File Manager in cPanel download your .htaccess file on your computer to make a back-up.

Step 2. From File Manager in cPanel open .htaccess file.

Step 3. Copy and paste from the provided file or type following lines into your .htaccess file:

#Disable Signature

ServerSignature OFF

Step 4. Save changes.

Step 5. Refresh the site.

This will disable your server's signature.

PROTECTING .HTACCES FILE

You also can protect .htaccess file itself. You use this file to protect everything, but you should protect it as well.

Step 1. From File Manager in cPanel download your .htaccess file on your computer to make a back-up.

Step 2. From File Manager in cPanel open .htaccess file.

Step 3. Copy and paste from the provided file or type following lines into your .htaccess file:

```
#Protect .htaccess file
<Files ~ "^.*\.([Hh][Tt][Aa])">
   order allow, deny
   deny from all
   satisfy all
</Files>
```

Step 4. Save changes.

Step 5. Refresh the site.

This expression says that any files that begin with .hta are not allowed for access. Another layer of security would be to use the code we used for securing config.php file for .htaccess file too:

```
# Preventing Access to .htaccess File
<Files .htaccess>
order allow,deny
deny from all
</Files>
```

CHAPTER 4. MORE SECURITY MEASURES

So far, we have WordPress installed, and we are using secure database with custom prefixes, secure passwords, we changed default admin name, added an array of security measures to .htaccess file. But we still need to add some more security layers.

DISABLE FILE EDITOR

In the WordPress dashboard, there are two places where as an administrator you can edit files. Go to Appearance>Editor (Fig19). This brings you to place where you can edit your theme's PHP code. On the right, you can see other files of the template. These PHP files comprise this theme, activated by default during the WordPress installation. If you choose any of these PHP files on the right, you can see that you have access to PHP code and can make whatever changes you want.

The second area where you can edit code is within the plugins. Go to Plugins>Editor, and you see another Editor submenu and PHP code of the plugin. As with the theme several PHP files comprise the plugin, what you are looking at is just one of them. This is another area that could be targeted by compromised administrative account. If you don't disable file editing hacked administrator account will be able directly insert the malicious code.

The aim of WordPress hack is to inject it with malware, include links to phishing websites, etc. To do this, hackers first launch brute force attack against WordPress site and once they get the password of WordPress administrator account, they log into WordPress dashboard from where they can use theme and plugin editors to access and modify files of activated theme and plugins.

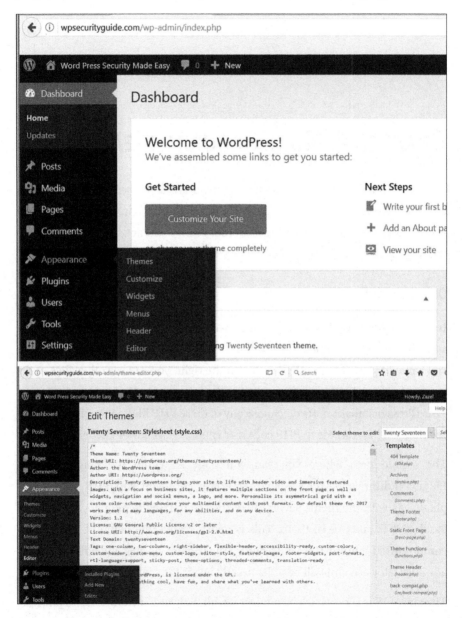

Figure 19. The two areas for editing PHP code.

By default, WordPress allows users with administrator role the ability to edit PHP files of plugins and themes inside the WordPress dashboard. This is usually the first thing the attacker would look for if they managed to gain access to the administrative account because this functionality allows modification of files and code execution on the server.

Given the security measures you have already employed we hope this won't happen but by disabling file editing, you are adding the further layer of protection between WordPress source code and the hackers, making impossible for them to modify any WordPress code directly from the WordPress dashboard.

For disabling file editing, you will need to edit wp-config.php file on your website by adding one line of code:

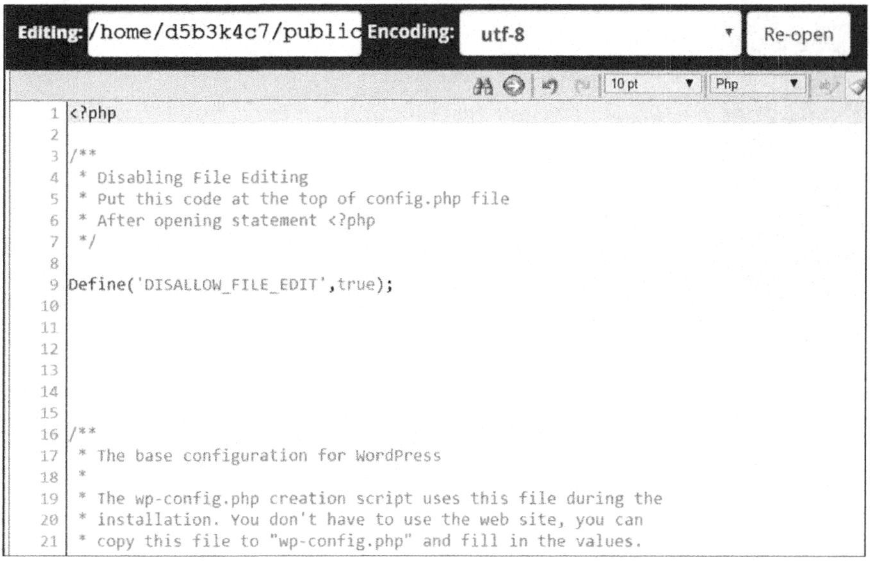
Editing: /home/d5b3k4c7/public
Encoding: utf-8
Re-open
10 pt
Php
<?php
/**
* Disabling File Editing
* Put this code at the top of config.php file
* After opening statement <?php
*/
Define('DISALLOW_FILE_EDIT',true);
/**
* The base configuration for WordPress
*
* The wp-config.php creation script uses this file during the
* installation. You don't have to use the web site, you can
* copy this file to "wp-config.php" and fill in the values.

Figure 20. Disabling editing from config.php file.

Step 1. From File Manager in cPanel download your wp-config.php file on your computer to make a back-up.

Step 2. From File Manager in cPanel open wp-config.php file by clicking Code Editor.

Step 3. The code must be put at the top of the config file, after the opening statement <?php, but above the line where MySQL settings are defined. Copy and paste from the provided file or type the following lines into your wp-config.php file (Fig.20):

#Disabling File Editing

Define('DISALLOW_FILE_EDIT', true);

Step 4. Save changes.

Step 5. Refresh the site.

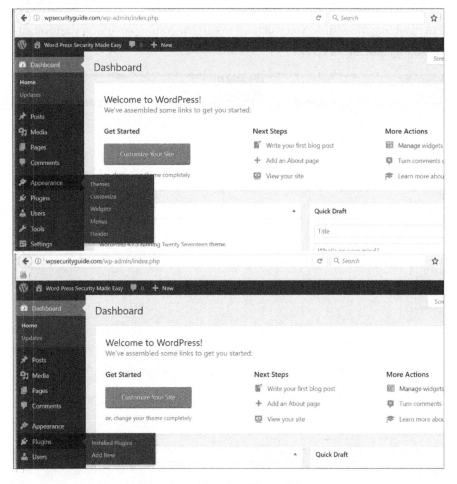

Figure 21. After disabling editing.

Now when you disabled file editing you'll see what effect it has within the dashboard. You have to log out and log back in your administrative account. If you check panel, you'll see that Editor submenus disappeared (Fig.21). Go to Appearance menu where you can see that Editor submenu has been removed entirely. And similar to Plugins. If somebody gains access to compromised administrative account, he/she can't see Editor submenu options to inject malicious code. So this is good security practice to follow. If you do need to modify or edit PHP file within the dashboard, you can temporarily re-enable file editing, but mostly I would leave it disabled.

DISABLING PHP ERROR REPORTING

WordPress is made up and requires a lot of PHP code to work, and by adding themes and plugins, users are adding more PHP code. After some time, different versions of WordPress, various versions of themes and plugins have to interact with each other, and sometimes something goes wrong if some PHP code is incompatible with your web server. Here comes error reporting. You get PHP error generated and displayed on the screen accessible for anybody visiting your website. Unless you turn off error reporting.

This error messages include information that is useful to hackers, like server path. Disabling the error reporting will prevent unauthorized eyes from seeing potentially sensitive information if something goes wrong.

Turning error reporting off is easy. You just need to add a small code to your wp-config.php file and you should put it above all other code lines in the file.

Step 1. From File Manager in cPanel download your wp-config.php file on your computer to make a back-up.

Step 2. From File Manager in cPanel open wp-config.php file by clicking Code Editor.

Step 3. The code must be put at the top of the config file, after the opening statement <?php, but above the line where MySQL settings are defined. Copy

and paste from the provided file or type following lines into your wp-config.php file (Fig.22):

#Disabling PHP Error Reporting

error_reporting(0);

Step 4. Save changes.

Step 5. Refresh the site.

Figure 22. Disabling Error Reporting.

Now error reports won't be displayed for everybody. If you find an error, you can always enable reporting to fix the problem and disable reporting again.

MOVING CONFIG.PHP

As we have seen during the installation, config.php file contains sensitive information, including details on accessing your WordPress database, database prefix, all your encryption codes, etc. Being afraid to leave this file in root directory of the WordPress installation is understandable.

According to some experts, one of the effective security measures is to protect this file by moving it to the folder one level above of WordPress installation directory. Some people say this is beneficial, others disagree. If you have WordPress installation in the root of your server or public_html folder you can follow this advice. But if you installed your WordPress in a separate folder then you can't do that because then your config file goes to public_html folder and it is accessible.

DON'T INFORM HACKERS

Hackers are always looking for vulnerabilities to get into your site. One way to do this is taking advantage of sites that are not updated to the latest version of WordPress. They can quickly look at WordPress security log to see whether the loopholes have been fixed and take advantage of sites that aren't staying up to date. They can do an automatic search for websites running these older versions. Unfortunately, information about WordPress version you are using is stored in your code and is extremally easy to find. Good news is this is easy to fix. You need to add few lines to your functions.php file, and you can do this manually.

There are few ways you can remove this tag, but this code is the best one (as I was assured) to use because you'll be removing it from your RSS feed as well. Ideally, you are always going to stay up-to-date with the latest version of WordPress to reduce any security risk, but this is just another layer of security.

Step 1. From File Manager in cPanel download your functions.php file on your computer to make a back-up.

Step 2. From File Manager in cPanel open functions.php file by clicking Code Editor.

Step 3. Copy and paste from the provided file or type following lines into your functions.php file:

```
//remove WordPress generator meta tag completely
function remove_generator_tag() {
return'';
}
Add_fitlter('the_generator','remove_generator_tag');
```
Step 4. Save changes.

Step 5. Refresh the site.

ARE HACKERS FINDING YOUR USERNAME?

Before moving forward create a couple of posts on your website. Content doesn't matter you can use some dummy text. We need them for demonstration purposes. We already talked about making usernames more unique and not using something generic like "admin" or your personal name. The idea was to not reveal your administrative username what is a half of the information hacker needs to get access to your WordPress site. Type into address bar your website name, forward slash, ?author=1, i.e. something like this: yourwebsite.com/?author=1. Hit Enter and see what happens.

You should see all of the posts of that particular author, and if you look at URL, you will see the author's username. And there is a huge chance that it is your administrative username. Now you can see how easy it is to find your administrative username if that is what you are using to log into your site. To avoid this, you can just create a non-administrative account for yourself to create posts, and also you want to make sure that you are hiding this a little better.

Now you are going to block this user name from being displayed for everyone. And if anybody does this type of search they will be redirected to your home page, and they are not going to see your username.

To prevent this from happening, you need to add a small code to functions.php file. Remember! Any mistake in the functions.php file can make your website stop working. This file is a core WordPress file and you have to be careful because one simple wrong move could make your entire site stop working.

Step 1. From File Manager in cPanel download your functions.php file on your computer to make a back-up.

Step 2. From File Manager in cPanel open functions.php file by clicking Code Editor.

Step 3. Copy and paste from the provided file or type following lines into your functions.php file:

```
add_action('template_redirect', 'bwp_template_redirect');
function bwp_template_redirect()
{
if (is_author())
{
wp_redirect( home_url() ); exit;
}
}
```

Step 4. Save changes.

Step 5. Refresh the site.

DON'T MAKE THEIR LIFE EASIER

You may have already noticed that if you type wrong username or password, WordPress is going to tell you what's wrong. If you enter the wrong username but correct password then WordPress is going to tell you that your username is incorrect, but the password is correct. If you type correct username but the wrong password it is going to inform you that your username is correct, but the password is incorrect. If that is helpful for you is also useful for hackers. Because now they know that one part of the equation they have right.

So, removing these login error messages makes harder for them to know if they have guessed any of the correct login information. For this, you will need to edit your functions.php file. To remove error messages from your login screen, you need to add following code to your theme's functions.php file:

Step 1. From File Manager in cPanel download your functions.php file on your computer to make a back-up.

Step 2. From File Manager in cPanel open functions.php file by clicking Code Editor.

Step 3. Copy and paste from the provided file or type following lines into your functions.php file:

//Remove Error Message from Login Page
// wp-content/themes/yourthemname/functions.php

add_filter('login_errors',create_function('$a', "return null;"));

Step 4. Save changes.

Step 5. Refresh the site.

Now if you try to log in and make a mistake you'll see that error message has been removed.

If you want just change error message, you should use the following code:

```
//Change Error Message On Login Page
// wp-content/themes/yourthemname/functions.php
function no_wordpress_errors(){
 return 'SOMETHING OR SOMEONE IS WRONG!';
}
add_filter( 'login_errors', 'no_wordpress_errors' );
```

You can put any text you like instead of - **SOMETHING OR SOMEONE IS WRONG!**.

FILE PERMISSIONS

Files and folders on your web server have assigned permissions. These permissions define who or what can access the files. Browsing files via FTP or your cPanel's File Manager, you may have noticed permission column with various numbers that define a different level of accessibility of those files. So, you need to double check your permissions to make sure they can't be accessed.

Let's look how to change these permissions so you can avoid having anyone upload or change your files. In cPanel's File Manager, you'll see the permission column, click on permission number and enter a new numeric value. And click save. Now you know how to change the number but what value should you change it into? What should you look for? Generally speaking, the lower the permission number, the more secure the file or directory is. And the more secure it is fewer people can access it including yourself.

What is you are looking for to make sure that absolutely nothing is set to 777. This file permission will allow hackers gain access to your files. They can modify any file, upload malicious code and take full control of your website. So that is something you should look for and stay away from.

If you are using shared server WordPress recommends wp-config.php file be set to 750.

Good practice is to use the most restrictive permission that works with your host.

All directories should be 755 (or 750)

All files should be 644(or 640)

Wp-config.php should be 644 (or 600)

If you want to know more about changing file permissions, you can find more information on WordPress.org.

CHAPTER 5. PREVENTING BRUTE FORCE ATTACKS

ABOUT THE BRUTE FORCE ATTACK

Brute force attack is very basic but widespread form of the hacker attack, using simple method to get access to your site. In just a matter of seconds a small software will randomly throw hundreds and thousands of username and password combinations at your site. The success rate of this form of attack is extremally high for accounts that have very insecure passwords or usernames. Worpdress.org has plenty of information about brute force attacks, and if interested you can learn more.

There are several effective methods to stop or prevent brute force attacks. If you like avoiding installing another plugin and don't mind few lines of code, we already discussed some of them in the chapter devoted to the .htaccess file, when we were talking about restriction of the admin area. If you haven't already done, you can insert in this code your IP address or of anybody else's as well who will access your site.

If you don't like putting codes in the .htaccess file or just want to add another layer of security to your WordPress site and don't mind adding some more plugins, let's discuss some of them.

GOOGLE CAPTCHA

CAPTCHA stands for "**C**ompletely **A**utomated **P**ublic **T**uring test to tell **C**omputers and **H**umans **A**part". To put it in plain English, a CAPTCHA is a program that protects sites from bots by creating tests that humans can easily pass but computer programs cannot. It is designed to protect websites from spam without actual human visitors, from malicious bots and abusive scripts. You may have seen these kinds of tests when logging into some sites you see a box to type into some skewed text consisting of letters and numbers. Unfortunately, advancements in bot intelligence are proving increasingly ineffective, so Google responded to this challenge by developing new captcha system where human just needs to tick a box. Simple, straightforward and efficient.

INSTALLATION

To add Google Captcha to your WordPress login page,

Step 1. Go to your WordPress dashboard and then Plugins>Add New

Step 2. In the Search Plugins field type "Google Captcha."

Step 3. Find Google CAPTCHA by BestWebSoft (Fig.23).

Step 4. Click Install Now. Wait for the installation to unpack and install

Step 5. Click Activate button.

Figure 23. Google CAPTCHA Installation. Step 3.

Set Up

Go to CAPTCHA>Settings. Before you can add Google Captcha to your WordPress login, you need to get the site key and secret key from Google Captcha service. Under the "Authentication" heading you will see "In order to use reCAPTCHA, please enter site and secret keys."

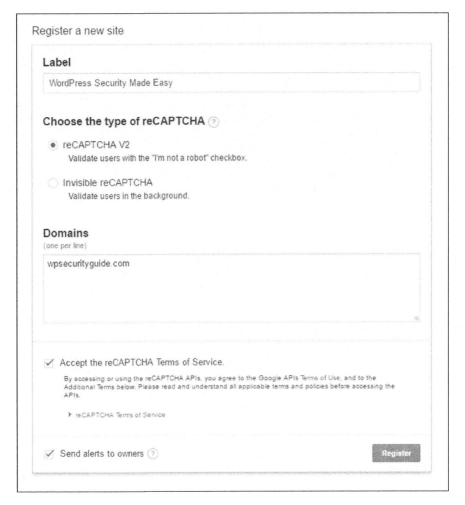

Figure 24. Registration form for CAPTCHA service.

You can manage your API keys here" link and click that link. It takes you to Google's captcha service. Here you need to log in with your Google account. And click "Get reCAPTCHA" button at the top. You need to register your web address.

In Label field enter the name of the site. In the Choose the type of reCAPTCHA (Fig.24), choose reCAPTCHA V2. In Domains fields add the domain name, yoursite.com. In Owners area put an email address to be notified of any alerts. Then click register. And it generates Site Key and Secret Key. Copy and paste site key and secret key back into your plugin on your WordPress dashboard.

Figure 25. Login page after CAPTCHA installation.

Leave all defaults and click Save Changes. If you log out of our WordPress dashboard and log in again. Now, you should see Google reCAPCHA on the login page (Fig.25). If you try to log in without ticking reCAPTCHA box, you'll get the Error message: You have entered incorrect CAPTCHA value. So, this is useful for deterring automated bots they won't be able to pass this stage, and this is another layer of security.

TWO FACTOR AUTHENTICATION

In this section, you will implement two-factor authentication process to defend your WordPress admin area. What that means is that website or application has two methods to be used to log in. A lot of sites have standard username and password and on the top of that have SMS message sent to cell phone or email to the inbox with a code a user has to type in. Essentially this is the sequence of the two different authentication processes. You try to get access with a username and password, this is the first authentication, and after that a code is sent to your mobile phone or inbox, which you need to enter into a form, this is the second authentication.

This process can be very annoying, but it adds an exceptional level of security to your site. If you want to add this measure of safety, there are lots of plugins that can do it for you.

We will install Two Factor Authentication (Google Authenticator) plugin. Why I chose this plugin? To be honest two most decisive factors for me were: first, it has email option for the second authentication, and second, it is easy to install. Besides, there are also some other factors that come after these two (again, for me, you must decide for yourself). For example, the plugin supports all types, and when say all I mean it, smartphones (iPhone, Android, BlackBerry), basic phones, landlines, etc.

The plugin supports multiple authentication methods along with their backup process and Two Factor for Woocommerce frontend login theme. What I discovered after installation and loved about this plugin was that it supports Device Identification function. You can select to remember device (your computer or laptop), and in the next login from the same device, you will not be prompted for Two Factor. It's a nice touch. You can have two-factor authentication without annoyance.

By default, Two-Factor Authentication (Google Authenticator) plugin for WordPress is free for one user forever. That means when you are installing the plugin you automatically install the free version and only after that, if you decide, can upgrade to paid version. In the free version only limited number of authentication methods are supported.

Figure 26. Installation. Step 3.

INSTALLATION

To install the plugin from your admin dashboard:

Step 1. Go to Plugins>Add New.

Step 2. In search field type: miniOrange 2 Factor Authentication

Step 3. Find plugin Google Authenticator – Two Factor Authentication (Fig.26).

Step 4. Click the Install Now button and then activate.

SETUP

On the dashboard go to miniOrange 2 Factor submenu. The first thing you see after activation is registration form with miniOrange, where you have to provide your email address and company name, by default, the form will use your domain name. Create the password and click Submit.

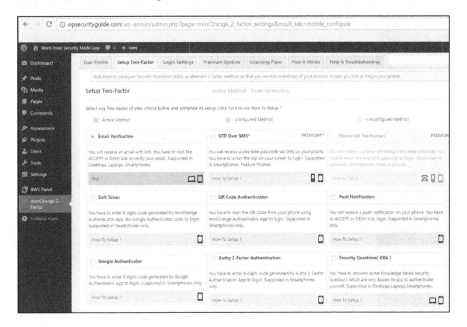

Figure 27. Setting Two Factor Configuration.

Next, you have to validate OTP by entering in field Enter OTP by entering one-time passcode sent to your email address. After entering six figure number click Validate OPT button.

Next, you are taken to Licensing Plans tab here you can compare free and premium plans and some additional information. Click OK. Got it button and move to Setup Two-Factor tab (Fig.27). Since we are not going to activate any other options and email verification is already activated you move to Login Settings (Fig.28).

Here you can make a choice in Select Login Screen Options section. Either Login with password + 2nd factor or Login with 2nd factor only. Enable "Remember Device" option. Make sure that Enable Two-Factor plugin box is checked and click Save Settings.

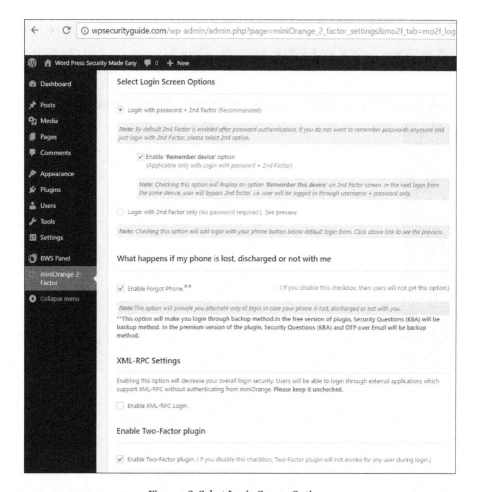

Figure 28. Select Login Screen Options.

Now plugin prompts you to log out and log in again. After you enter login credentials plugin prompts you again that an email has been sent to your address and they are waiting for your approval.

When you open designated email, you will see the following message:

Dear Customer,

You initiated a transaction WordPress 2 Factor Authentication Plugin:

To accept, Accept Transaction

To deny, Deny Transaction

Thank you,

miniOrange Team

You just need to click Accept Transaction link, and you have one last step to make. Plugin prompts following: question Do you want to remember this device? (Fig. 29). Click yes only if it's your personal computer and only you have access to it.

Figure 29. Remember your device.

Now you have the two-factor authentication. As I mentioned you can use SMS messaging option as well, but we are not going to discuss this option.

CHAPTER 6. INSTALL & CONFIGURE SECURITY PLUGIN

SECURITY PLUGINS, WHY WORDFENCE?

Limiting the installation of too many plugins is a good security practice. However, in some instances, plugins are necessary for the safety of your websites. You can find few superb security plugins, with different levels of difficulty of installation and setup process, and a different number of features in free version vs. number of features in paid version. Wordfence is the one that offers so much security with its free version that I even don't consider upgrading to paid version. Combined with other security measures discussed in this guide Wordfence provides formidable level of protection possible for your WordPress website for free.

Wordfence covers five main components of security areas: scanning, detecting, protecting, blocking, repairing. If you compare features of free and paid versions, you'll see that free version offers most of the features that paid version does. For those who is looking for an economical and simple way of protecting their WordPress website, the Wordfence free version is simply the excellent choice.

WORDFENCE INSTALLATION

Let's now turn to our dashboard and install and configure Wordfence plugin.

Figure 30. Wordfence Installation. Step 3.

Step 1. In your WordPress Dashboard go to Plugins>Add New

Step 2. In Search Plugin field (upper right corner of the browser) enter Wordfence.

Step 3. Find Wordfence Security plugin (Fig.30).

Step 4. Click Install Now and wait for package to download,

Step 5. Click Activate button and enter your email to get critical alerts from Wordfence.

WORDFENCE CONFIGURATION

In your WordPress admin dashboard on the left-hand panel at the bottom, you should see Wordfence's sub-menu, click it once. Wordfence submenu offers lots of options many of them monitoring and checking the state of your Wordfence plugin. The main submenu is "Options" if you click it you can see the whole array of choices and thick boxes. We are going to go through many of them. If you need more information, you can always click small information buttons next to each option heading with "i" in the center. In the following sections if I don't mention some of the options that you can see on your screen it means don't change default setting.

FIREWALL SETUP

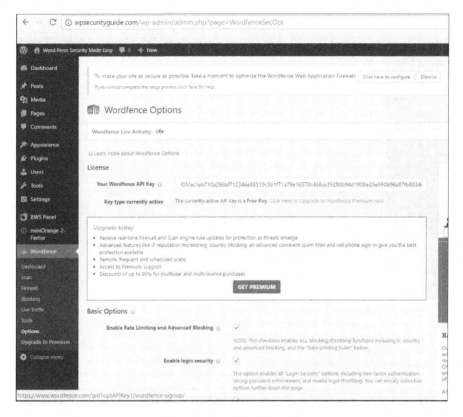

Figure 31. Installing Firewall.

At the top of WordPress admin page, right after installation, you will see "To make your site as secure as possible, take a moment to setup the Wordfence Web Application Firewall." Click the "Click here to configure" button (Fig.31), and the configuration page will detect the server configuration for your site. On the next screen click the Continue button.

The next page most likely will recommend downloading .htaccess or .user.ini for backup. You can upload the backup files to your site if there are any problems. Once you have downloaded the files, click Continue button.

On the next screen click Save button to save settings and to complete the firewall setup. To continue Wordfence setup go to Wordfence>Options.

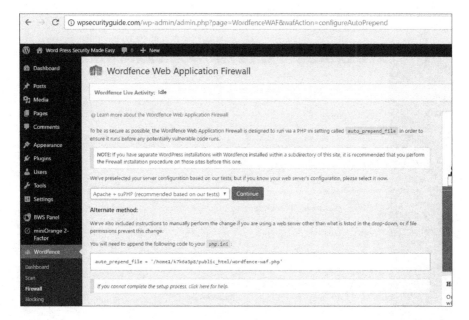

Figure 32. Installing firewall, continued.

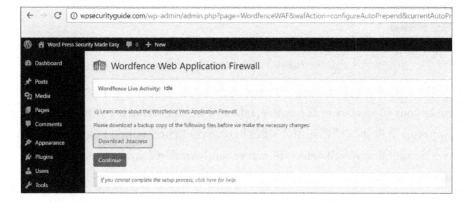

Figure 33. Installing firewall, continued.

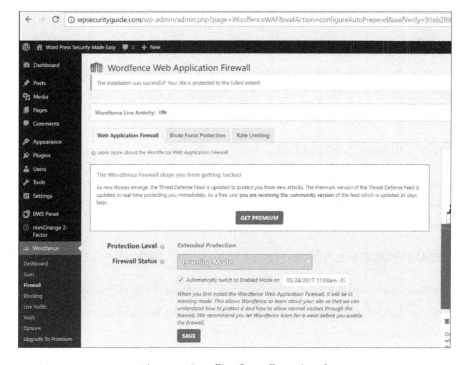

Figure 34. Installing firewall, continued.

WORDFENCE API KEY

You don't need to do anything with this option. Your Wordfence API key serves two functions: 1. It allows Wordfence servers to uniquely identify your WordPress installation; 2. Wordfence plugin on your site will contact Wordfence's servers and automatically retrieves a free API key which allows you to avoid visiting their site and register your plugin.

BASIC OPTIONS

Most of the basic options are for paid version, and we discuss only those of them which are for the free version.

ENABLE LOGIN SECURITY

This option is a global switch for items that appear under the heading "Login Security" further down on the options page. You should enable it.

Enable Live Traffic View

You should not choose this option only if you are using extremally low-cost hosting plan with extremally limited resources available. If this is the case, you can reduce the load on your site by disabling live traffic. And considering changing plan or host will be a good idea.

Enable Automatic Scheduled Scans

Enabling this option is a must. For free version plugins, scans occur once a day, and Wordfence chooses exactly when to scan in 24 hour periods. But you can perform manual scan any time you like.

Update Wordfence Automatically When A New Version Is Released

We have discussed the importance of timely updates for the security of our site. This is especially important for security plugins like Wordfence. So you should enable this option.

Where To Email Alerts

Usually, this must be WordPress site administrator's email address and you can, if needed, add several email addresses separated by commas.

How Does Wordfence Get IPs?

Most websites will work fine using the default configuration. You can read more about which addresses Wordfence considers private in the help file.

ADVANCED OPTIONS

Alerts

In this section, there are 13 choices, and they are pretty much self-explanatory. The alerts will be sent to the email address you provided in "Basic Options" in the field with the heading "Where to email alerts."

Good policy is if you are only emailed when there is a critical problem that requires your attention. Configure these options so that you are alerted to critical issues - only items that should require your hands-on intervention. My suggestion is tick all of them except two: "Alert me when someone with administrator access signs in," and "Only alert me when that user signs in from a new device or location," otherwise your inbox will be flooded with email alerts.

I recommend deselecting "Alert me when someone with administrator access signs in" because whenever you are signing in your account it will immediately send an email, and it gets into your inbox even before you finished login process. If you don't have users on your website or don't allow registrations, then option "Alert me when non-admin user signs in" might be interesting for you. Otherwise, you might be annoyed on a regular basis.

Email Summary

If you enable email summary, Wordfence will email your summary of all activities using the selected frequency. Make sure option "Enable activity report widget on dashboard" is activated, this is very crucial thing for monitoring your website

Live Traffic View

If you have live traffic enabled in Basic Options, then this gives you a few more items you can customize including the ability to ignore specific users or specific IP addresses or browsers. I wouldn't change anything here.

Scans to Include

In this block, I would enable all of the options except the following: "Enable HIGH SENSITIVITY scanning (may give false positives)" and "Use low resource scanning (reduces server load by lengthening the scan duration)." Leave as it is following three: "Exclude files from a scan that match these wildcard patterns (one per line)," "Limit the number of issues sent in the scan results email" and "Time limit that a scan can run in seconds."

Wordfence recommends leaving the option "Enable HIGH SENSITIVITY scanning (may give false positives)" turned off. Only if you are using plugin to clean site, then you can enable this, and it may help you find source of a glitch.

Unless you have very cheap host with very limited resources at your disposal you should avoid enabling "Use low resource scanning (reduces server load by lengthening the scan duration)" this may make scans to take 2-4 times longer.

Make sure that option "Scan core files against repository versions for changes" and "Scan theme files against repository versions for changes" are enabled because these are enabling scanning theme and plugin files against repository versions for changes. It means that if you have standard WordPress plugins and themes installed from the WordPress repository then Wordfence can scan these files and if there is anything that is not supposed to be there like changed file, code, etc., then it will send alert. This is crucial because when hackers try to enter your site, they might change some data and include some code in several places. In this case, Wordfence will send you an alert to look into and take some actions.

Enabling "Scan files outside your WordPress installation" is always a good idea. On your server, there are files outside of your WordPress installation as well, and a hacker can get access to your server, and when he doesn't manipulate WordPress itself, you will not know about it until it's too late, so activate this and you will get a message whenever that happens.

"Scan images, binary, and other files as if they were executable" you should enable this option as well because your media directory is one of the most critical things you need to protect if you have users on your website and they can upload user avatar, logo, or image. Hacker might upload something that looks like an image but has some hidden code, and it is executable. You want to avoid this.

RATE LIMITING RULES

Wordfence includes a rate limiting firewall that controls how your site content can be accessed. In older versions, heading of this block was Firewall Rules. You should enable "Immediately block fake Google crawlers," this is good defense if people are stealing your content and pretending to be Google bots as they crawl your site. This option will immediately block anyone faking to be Google.

But make sure that option "How should we treat Google's crawlers" is enabled. This allows verified Google crawlers to have unlimited access to your site because they are indexing your website and if you don't let their search bot to index your site then your site will not be included in the Google search.

For the following options, I'll just give you choices I made based on WordPress recommendations:

If anyone's requests exceed – 240 per minute (4 per second)-block it

If a crawler's page views exceed – 120 per minute (2 per second) – throttle it

If a crawler's pages not found (404s) exceed – Unlimited-throttle it

If a human's page views exceed – 30 per minute (1 every 2 seconds) – throttle it

If a human's pages not found (404s) exceed – 10 per minute (1 every 6 seconds) – block it

If 404s for known vulnerable URLs exceed – 4 per minute (1 every 15 seconds)- block it

How long is an IP address blocked when it breaks a rule – 1 month

LOGIN SECURITY OPTIONS

For "Enforce strong passwords" Wordfence recommends option "Force admins and publishers use strong passwords."

For "Lock out after how many login failures" Wordfence recommends you to set this number up to 20, but I never set more than 3.

"Lock out after how many forgot password attempts" Wordfence recommends tthat setting this to 5 should be sufficient for most sites.

"Count failures over what time period" - this specifies the period you count failures over. So if you specify 5 minutes and 20 failures then if someone fails to sign in 20 times during a 5 minute period, they will be locked out from login.

Brute force attacks usually send one login attempt every few seconds. So if you have set the number of login failures to 20, then 5 minutes is plenty of time to catch a brute force hack attempt. You do have the option to set it higher. The amount of time a user is locked out I always put maximum time.

As Wordfence states the option "Immediately lock out invalid usernames" was requested by many members or Wordfence community. It is an excellent security measure, but you have to be cautious, because your real users will be blocked out as well, if they miss-type their username.

Dashboard Notification Options

In this section, I would recommend ticking all the boxes available for the free version users.

Other Options

"Whitelisted IP addresses that bypass all rules" This might be your IP address. If you put your IP address here, you cannot be accidentally blocked out from your WordPress, what might happen if you usually log in from different computers and IP addresses and are prone to forget log out. Only use this feature if you are sure you have a permanent IP address because some people don't (depending on the type of connection).

Hide WordPress version – We already talked that WordPress by default discloses what its version is. This option will hide it from outsiders. But Wordfence doesn't recommend enabling this since there are other methods of determining the WordPress version.

"Block IPs who send POST requests with blank User-Agent and Referrer, this is against brute force hacking scripts sending login attempts and comment spam attempts, so you want to make sure you have this enabled.

If you want to export all these settings safely to your other sites, Wordfence will give you token number you will copy and paste in an entirely different site where you have Wordfence installed. You need to paste this token in Import Settings field and you are done.

Now when you have your Wordfence installed and basic setting set up, you can go to the dashboard again.

CHAPTER 7. BACKUP AND SITE RESTORATION

IMPORTANCE OF BACKUP

Another crucial aspect of the security of your website is to keep current backups. You need reliable backup system in place whether you are doing it manually or using plugin that can do it for you. Instead of doing whenever you have time, security wise scheduled backups are better idea. It's easier and more efficient if you have some program that lets you run the backup in time intervals defined according to your needs.

Backup allows you to get back your site after hacking or malicious bot attacks. These are typical cases when an attack makes your website ugly or entirely unresponsive. As site owners, we can be the threat as well. We make mistakes, sometimes delete something by mistake or mess with PHP code. Sometimes we don't make mistakes, but anyway getting disaster when trying to update themes, plugins, or even WordPress core itself. Installation of new plugins or themes is not an exception as well. Whatever the case, the backup can be used to retract any files and databases to restore your website to pre-disaster state.

Sometimes, you need to migrate web hosting provider, or it shuts down. Again, recent backup enables you to restore website to another provider with a simple nameserver changes with your domain registrar and in no time your site is back and running.

It is not wise and secure to be entirely dependent on web hosts in this vital aspect of security. You shouldn't assume that hosting provider does backups for you.

Can you be sure that your hosting provider makes regular backups of your site? How often? How can they be restored? How long will it take? To be realistic, if you don't make and store your backups, you have no control. More importantly, do you want to leave the safety of your site only in the hands of your hosting company? Bottom line: take full control of when backups are made, how often and where they are stored.

WHAT FILES COMPRISE WORDPRESS

Before we continue, it will be helpful to refresh yourself about building blocks of your WordPress site. Typical WordPress site consists of following items: WordPress core installation (composed by files and directories, usually located in your web root directory, for example, /public_html which we have seen on our host); WordPress Plugins; WordPress Themes; Images and Files; PHP and other code files, and WordPress database.

BACKUP PLUGIN OVERVIEW

Now, you are going to install the backup plugin which works very well with WordPress. It is called UpdraftPlus. Similar to Wordfence and other plugins, there is a paid and free version. We are going to install free version to make it as economical as promised.

UpdraftPlus offers multiple storage options that you can set up as destinations for your backup files. By default, UpdraftPlus creates backups and stores them locally on your WordPress website. This approach is excellent for quick and convenient restores you might need to perform. But you must have an off-site backup so you have a second copy stored in case your hosting provider closes down or you have issues accessing default storage on your site. Either way, security wise the second backup sent to remote storage is a must.

If you use the free version, don't use FTP because it is not encrypted. I suggest you start with Dropbox, Google Drive or S3. If you use these options as a backup destination the connection will be encrypted by default.

UpdraftPlus backs up essentially everything, your database, and all WordPress content, meaning your uploads, plugins, themes, and additional files created by plugins. The free version does not support backup of the core WordPress itself, but this is not essential since you can always download it again. Later in this chapter we will discuss how to recover the whole site with free edition without resorting to paid premium version.

BACKUP PLUGIN – INSTALLATION AND CONFIGURATION

Now you are going to install and configure UpdraftPlus plugin file.

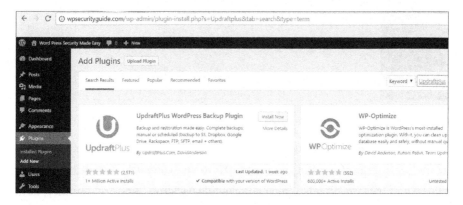

Figure 35. UpdraftPlus installation, Step 2.

Step 1. In your Dashboard go to Plugins>Add New.

Step 2. Go to the upper right-hand field which says Search Plugins and type UpdraftPlus. And the first result must be UpdraftPlus Back Up and Restoration plugin (Fig.35).

Step 3. Click "Install Now." Wait for unpackaging of installation files.

Step 4. Click Activate button.

Now if you go to Dashboard>Settings you will see the new submenu called "UpdraftPlus Backups." If you click that, you are taken to configuration options. Now you need to configure a couple of settings.

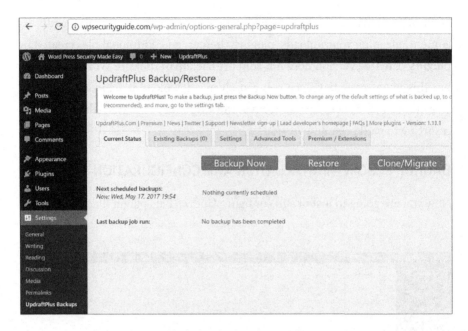

Figure 36. Current Status tab.

Let's first quickly run through tabs. First one is "Current Status" (Fig.36), which is the central dashboard of the plugin. Here you can click "Backup Now "and start a new backup job. Also, you can schedule backups. "Restore" button is used to perform restores. "Clone/Migrate" button this goes to more advanced backup and recovery methods and also requires the premium license, so we are not going to discuss it.

Next, we have the quick summary of "Next Scheduled Backups," it shows When next scheduled backup is due to take place. There are no backups planned yet so for the moments it must say - Nothing currently scheduled. Last backup job run will say when last backup job was run, and the link to the log file which stores messages. For now, it says No backup has been completed.

Now let's go to "Settings" tab (Fig.37). And we see here two options. File and database backup intervals. I can't recommend what to put in here for your website. Every site is different, has different purposes, has content that is more dynamic or more static. Also, the number of backups to be retained depends on how far back you want to go if you need to restore your site and how much of storage space each backup takes. To give an example of what I do for some of my websites where I may add content once or twice a week I set weekly backup schedule. And keep at least four weeks' worth of backups retained. I also keep file and database backups same, at the same interval to ensure I point in time consistent backup.

"Include in files backup" option reminds you the earlier section where you were reminded about what files exactly free plugin backs up. It includes plugins, themes, Uploads (excludes previous backups), and any other directories found inside wp-content. Next look at "Email," tick this box to have the basic backup report sent to your site admin address. Go to the bottom and click "Save Changes." And you have configuration done.

CONNECTING BACKUP TO CLOUD STORAGE

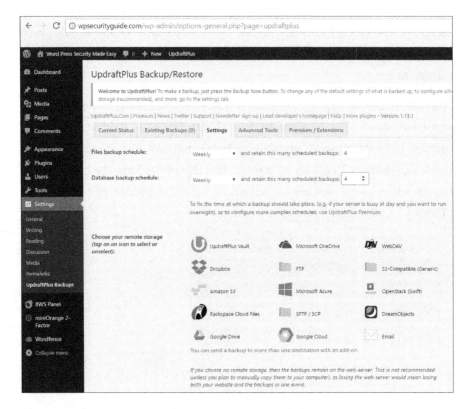

Figure 37. Remote storage choice.

Now, it's time to connect UpdraftPlus backup to the remote storage provider. For demonstration purposes, we are going to use Dropbox, but you can choose any options available.

Step 1. Go to Setting>UpdraftPlus Backups and go to the settings tab.

Step 2. Down the page, you see "Choose your remote storage. (tap on an icon to select or unselect)" and beneath of icons you read: If you choose no remote storage, then the backups remain on the web-server. This is not recommended (unless you plan to copy them to your computer manually), as losing web-server would mean losing both your website and the backups in one event."

Figure 38. Choosing Dropbox as remote storage.

Step 3. Choose Dropbox (Fig.38).

Step 4. Read carefully the following notes from UpdraftPlus:

> Dropbox is a great choice because UpdraftPlus supports chunked uploads – no matter how big your site is. UpdraftPlus can upload it a little at a time, and not get thwarted by timeouts."

> Good news your sites communication with Dropbox can be encrypted. If you see any errors to do with encryption, then look in the Expert Setting for more help.

> Need to use sub-folder? Backups are saved in apps/UpdraftPlus. If you back up several sites into the same Dropbox and want to organize with sub-folders, then there's an add-on for that.

Authenticate with Dropbox: after you have saved your setting by clicking "Save Changes" below, then come back here once and click this link to complete authentication.

Step 5. Go down and click "Save Changes".

Step 6. Go back to the settings tab and click the link Authenticate with Dropbox.

Step 7. Follow the link in pop-up window Remote Storage Authentication (Fig.39).

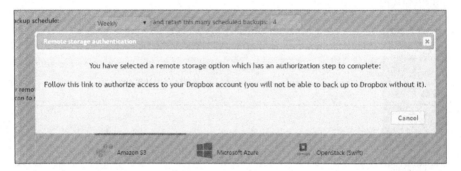

Figure 39. Remote storage authentication link.

Step 8. Next, you see on the screen: UpdraftPlus would like access to its own folder, Apps>UpdraftPlus, inside your Dropbox. Click "Allow." Now you can see that UpdraftPlus created Apps folder with UpdraftPlus subfolder in it and there is nothing there. This is the place where backup files will be stored.

Switch back to the dashboard. And go to "Current status" tab. Take the manual backup. Click Backup Now button, include Database, Files, and send this backup to remote storage. Which is now ticked by default. In the next window click down "Backup Now" button. And you can see a progress bar. Wait for backup to complete. When you can see it says, "Uploading files to remote storage" (Fig. 40). It means backups have already been taken and now being uploaded to remote storage. So, backup was successful and now is complete. If you go to your Dropbox folder, Apps >UpdraftPlus, you can see different zip files of your backup.

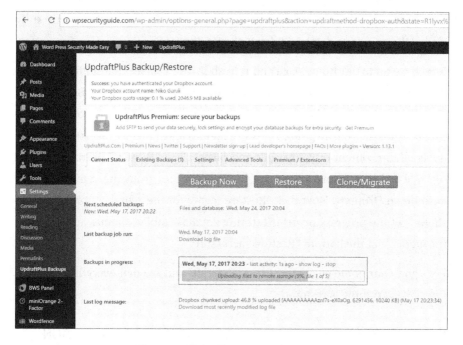

Figure 40. Uploading to remote storage.

It means now your backups are safely stored on remote cloud storage and if you do lose your website and you've taken local backups you always have your remote backups in your cloud storage.

MINI DISASTER SIMULATION AND RECOVERY

In this section, you are going to simulate a mini disaster. The moment when you just realized that you either deleted some content, or hacker has done this. Either way, you realize that you have a problem when you need to restore the site from the backup. So, you are going to delete a page you've set up for demo post, and theme's folder to make it more realistic. Then you will restore latest backup from the remote storage you've created earlier.

In dashboard go Pages>All Pages and go to Posts and you see all posts that you've created. Mark some posts, and delete. Go to Pages and delete all pages. Go to your file manager and public_html web root directory and drop down /wp-content/themes. You should see your active theme directory. This is currently loaded theme on your site, just delete theme directory.

Now if we go to our home page and refresh it, you can see that nothing at all is there. So, let's go back to your dashboard Settings>UpdraftPlus Backups and click "Restore" button. And you'll go to the latest backup. Click "Restore" button. And in this case, you are going to restore themes and database, because database holds all the content of your pages and posts. Click "Restore" button. And you see that it is retrieving and preparing backup files from the remote storage location on Dropbox. Now click "Restore" again for the actual restore. Next you should get the progress report. Restoring database tables, themes and you have the message at the bottom "Restore successful."

Let's go to our home page now. Press "Refresh" and see that everything is back. Check if everything is restored.

FULL DISASTER RECOVERY WITH UPDRAFTPLUS FREE EDITION

Now let's discuss what you need for complete disaster recovery when using UpdraftPlus Free Edition. If you remember, the premium edition backs up everything in your web root directory which includes WordPress core files and core files are not backed up with the free version. So, again looking at economical versus functionality to execute full disaster recovery with the free edition you will need:

1. To install WordPress again;
2. To install UpdraftPlus plugin again;
3. Reconnect to your Remote Storage that you used to backup to
4. Restore all the components Database, Plugins, Themes, Uploads, Others (all directories and files within wp-content directory)
5. Upload backed up copy of wp-config.php (make sure you are using hosting provider's cPanel's file manager);
6. Upload backup copy of .htaccess;
7. Upload backup copy of functions.php.

As you can see for full recovery of your site you need two types of resources:

1. Resources you always can access and download from the internet: WordPress installation package and UpdraftPlus;
2. AND resources you already should have prepared if you followed this guide: 1. Back up files on remote storage and access to it; 2. Copy of config.php backup file; 3. Copy of .httaccess.txt back up file; 4. Copy of functions.php back up file.

BEFORE YOU GO

THANK YOU SO MUCH for checking out **WordPress Security Made Easy**. I know you could have picked from dozens of books on Amazon. But you took a chance with my guide. So, big thanks for buying this book and reading all the way to the end.

If you liked what you've read, if it was useful, then I need your help. Please take a moment to leave a review for this book on Amazon. If you leave a review, it will make this guide sound better for other WordPress users who need it. If you'd be willing to post even just a short sentence or two, I'd really appreciate it.

This feedback will help me continue to write the kind of books that help you get results. And if you love it, then please let me know.

All the best,

Niko

Found Typos in this book?

If you do find any typos or grammatical errors in this book, I'd be very grateful if you could let me know using this email address:

typo@wpsecurityguide.com

Made in United States
North Haven, CT
12 October 2022